HISTORY OF THE MALTESE

Long ago, perhaps as far back as 6000 BC, there was a small white domesticated dog known generally as the "little white dog of antiquity." Today, this little fellow is thought to be the direct lineal ancestor of several contemporary breeds as well as identifiable rare regional breeds, some extinct. These include the Bichon Frise or Bichon a Poil Frise or the Canary Bichon; the little Lion dog or Bichon Petit Chien Leon; the Havanese Bichon or Havana silk dog; and the Bolognese dog. Another, and the most prominent of breeds in this category, is the Maltese, known to the ancients of the Greco-Roman world as the Melita Dog, from their word for Malta.

There is considerable evidence that the little Maltese is the closest of all to the "little white dog of antiquity" and may be essentially the same dog. Charles Darwin himself estimated the Maltese to be of the time-honored date mentioned above—6000 BC. If this is true, then it is fair to say that the Maltese is much more than the cousin of the other breeds; he is, in fact, their ancestor. Each of the other breeds bears a strong resemblance to the Maltese but has characteristics that distinguish it from the Maltese. These unique characteristics were once probably present to some degree in the Maltese itself. They proved in all likelihood attractive enough

The Maltese has an illustrious history and is one of the few canines that is always associated with the privileged and affluent.

and valuable enough to encourage continuous selective breeding, which continued to the point where a new offshoot breed was created. In this way we may account for the family of small, mostly white dogs that constitute the Bichon family. This thesis permits us to reconcile the little white dog of antiquity with the panoply of regional small white dogs mentioned, and the ancient Maltese. They are all in their way direct descendants of the old model Maltese, known to our Greco-Roman forebears as the dog of Malta.

When we think of Malta, the small island situated in the eastern Mediterranean between Sicily and Libya, several things come to mind. An island fortress and British Naval base, it was held against seemingly hopeless odds during the second World War.

Our earliest likenesses of the Maltese are from Egypt and Greece. There is a statue of a Maltese-like dog recovered from a dig near Cairo, Egypt, which has been dated from 600 BC to 300 BC, putting it close to or within the Ptolemaic time of Greek influence in Egypt. Certainly it is within the time of trade and commerce with the eastern Mediterranean sea-faring peoples.

Whatever interpretation we give the Egyptian connection, the first true record of the Maltese as a prized pet occurred with the ancient Greeks. The Greeks were the first to portray them as pets, both in art and verse. The philosopher Aristotle wrote a short history and account of the breed, which by his time had become associated with and named for the island of Malta. Aristotle gives the island of Malta as the source or place of origin for the breed but it is likely that the Maltese of old, if he is the original or close to the original little white dog of antiquity, really comes from central Europe and was brought south to the Eastern Mediterranean by migrating peoples and merchant traders. He may well have been brought to Malta by the Phoenicians, since Malta was an important trading center centuries before Aristotle's time. It is certain that whenever and however it was brought to Malta, the island was not, as Aristotle believed, its original home. Rather, it was a stepping stone and stepping off place for the little white dogs as they made their way eastward and westward across the centuries to the eastern and western reaches of the Mediterranean and the known ancient world.

Certainly, as with other regional breeds, the dog that remained in Malta continued to develop unique qualities in isolation from other regions. (The Bichon "cousins" that were taken to other areas developed characteristics unique to their regions.) It is likely that there were fewer changes in the dog from Malta, and it is in this sense that the Maltese is closest to, if not the original bichon dog. Malta rightfully deserves to give its name to the beautiful little breed we know as the Maltese. After all, Malta is

Puffery and pampering have always been major parts of a Maltese's life.

where the closest clones stabilized and flourished. Since the little white dog in its accepted form was known to the ancients as the Maltese and this rough standard was bred to their satisfaction in Malta, then they were entirely justified in naming the little white breed the Maltese.

There is evidence that the Maltese-type dog migrated well beyond the eastern Mediterranean and may indeed be part of the foundation stock for several eastern breeds, including the ancestors of the Lhasa Apso and the Pekingese. This is all conjecture, and is deduced from sketchy resemblances and speculations passed down through time.

We need not speculate about the Maltese in classic Greece in the late Hellenic and early Hellenistic periods because they are commemorated again and again in Greek literature. The Greeks and later the Romans, both of whom called the dogs Maltese and assumed their place of origin to be Malta, made and kept these dogs as pets. They were pampered and treated much the same as the lap dogs of the privileged are today. They were especially popular with upper-class women and the wives of the wealthy and powerful. These ladies spoiled them with the finest foods and gave them every comfort. Living in the lap of luxury, celebrated in Greek literature and commemorated on shrines, pottery and other objects of art, it is easy to see that the Maltese were considered very valuable.

As with most prized possessions, the Maltese didn't come cheap. They were very expensive and not for everyone. They were transported with great care by merchant traders and became a valuable commodity to be sent and traded to the far corners of the Greco-Roman world. Merchants and traders knew that there was a market for these little white dogs among the wealthy, and they were gingerly transported to maintain their value.

Consequently, the Maltese was loved and cherished in the ancient world like few others. Later, in a time of great cruelty and brutality during the Roman era, the Maltese continued to be a precious object much beloved by its patrician owners. The Maltese is documented in detail in Roman writing. The Maltese was described by the Romans as a very small dog of the type kept as a pet. We know he had a long silky coat similar to today's Maltese. The little white pet continued to be popular with the rich and powerful. Roman Emperors, including the savant, Claudius, owned them.

It is recorded that a Roman governor in the first century owned a beautiful little Maltese whom he loved dearly. The story of his love for his little pet is preserved touchingly in the poetry of the period. Wall frescoes from excavated Roman ruins supplement the detailed written records, poems, and other prose of the Roman period in their portrayal of the tiny dog.

By the end of the first century, the little Maltese had been bred down to a tiny size, some as small as a ferret, and weighing only a few pounds. Their position as a constant companion of Roman gentry, especially the ladies, put a premium on small size. They were carried everywhere, even into the Roman baths, and treasured as ornaments and caste markers. Their tiny size made them nearly as portable as precious jewels, and almost as valuable. The smaller the Maltese was, the more it suited the noble Roman woman who could have her lightweight, constant companion with her at all times. The dog could even be kept in the folds of a heavy gown or a well-buttressed bosom, and there are Roman accounts confirming that it was! It was as this high status item with enormous snob appeal that the Maltese spread around the Roman empire.

Around this same time an early form of standardization of the Maltese was developed, if only in the sense of small size and coat. A rather primitive standard, but one nonetheless. It was also at this time that a rough-and-tumble market value was established for the Maltese by the merchant traders serving the needs of the rich and powerful. Thus it might be fair to say that this was a historical first, since it is likely this was the first time that a breeder's market price was established throughout a wide geographical area for some kind of desirable standard of dog. The Egyptians had their Salukis but they weren't traded as commodities. It was in the Greco-Roman world, with its international cosmopolitan markets, that this early form of dog commerce was established. With some poetic license, then, we can say that the first commercial breeding program of a known breed began with the Maltese or his close ancestor. This makes the Maltese the granddaddy of all standard breeds and, collaterally, of all show dogs.

When Rome weakened and split into eastern and western empires, the Maltese disappeared in the west. It continued to flourish for a time in Byzantine society. With the spread of Islam and the gradual shrinking of the Byzantine Empire, the breed seemingly vanished and remained obscure through the Dark Ages in Europe. Apparently the barbaric tribes that sacked Rome and populated western Europe were civilized enough to value the company of this prized little pet, for the Maltese surfaced again in the middle ages—in its original form—and is well documented in accounts from all parts of Europe, east and west.

As Byzantium shrank and was gradually displaced by the Ottoman Empire, the Turkish sultans found a home for the Maltese in their palaces and their harems. Thus the little Maltese survived on the margin of Europe during the Dark Ages and was very much alive and well and easily absorbed back into Europe. The Ottoman Empire may have well been a transit point for trade and transportation of the Maltese between east and west, as there are writings about the Maltese in the Orient in the late Middle Ages. With the renaissance in Europe, which brought a rebirth of learning and culture, as well as an interest in luxury and creative comforts, came the rediscovery of the value of pets.

The flowering of literature and art during the Renaissance bore heavy witness to the presence of the Maltese; the dog appears again and again. This was true all through western Europe, but especially in France, where the Maltese appears often in the celebrated tapestries of the 14th century. It appears frequently in the Renaissance literature of France, where it is often referred to as the Lyonaise Bichon or the dog of Lyon. While a regional form of the Maltese undoubtedly developed a distinct identity at this time, Lyon was not where the species originated, and the dog depicted in the tapestries and described in letters is clearly the Maltese.

Whatever the breed's origin, be it central Europe before the dawn of civilization, the ancient trading center of Malta or Lyon, as was mistakenly believed in the Middle Ages, it was in England that the Maltese was refined.

The Maltese was first imported to England from Lyon during the time of Henry VIII. It was

The Maltese, one of the most popular breed of lap dogs, has been known to pop up in the most unlikely of places.

Elizabeth, Henry's daughter, frequently portrayed with lap dogs, who was the first European monarch to definitely own a Maltese, a gift from the Sultan of Turkey. Her arch rival and cousin, Mary Queen of Scots, was another. Undoubtedly influenced by her cousin and following fashion, Mary is known to have imported Maltese from Lyon, one of which accompanied her to her execution by Elizabeth—perhaps an early example of competition amidst dog fanciers.

Elizabeth's physician, who wrote possibly the first breed classification of types of dogs existing in any country, listed the Maltese as a breed known in England. He described the

Maltese as being very small and gentle, adored by women as a constant companion, and, as with the ancients, more desirable the smaller it was and the easier to carry.

The Elizabethan period in England was one of expanded commerce and seafaring mercantile activity. The Maltese as bred in England was traded in markets as far off as China, where the breed is recorded in archives and in art. Apparently, at this time—the late 16th and early 17th centuries—there were two varieties of Maltese, a longhaired and a short, wirehaired type. Earlier tapestries, especially those of the French from the early 14th century, depict both, with the longhaired type looking almost exactly like the contemporary Maltese. In the 17th and 18th centuries, the descriptions became more detailed and certain traits were described with greater frequency and consistency. In time, the long, silky-coated type dominated, and the wirehaired type gradually disappeared.

Again and again reference is made in the 17th and 18th centuries to the strong preference and bias for small size. As in ancient Rome and Greece, writers of the time alluded to the popularity of the tiny Maltese with upper-class and rich ladies of fashion who carried the dogs as fashion accessories. It was fashionable in Mary Stuart's time to carry Maltese in the folds of garments, including sleeves or special pouches sewn into shirts and dresses. Indeed, Mary's dog was carried in this way at the luckless queen's beheading. As in former times, this practice and others put a premium on tininess; the smaller the dog and the more delicately formed, the more valuable. Over time, the Maltese became synonymous with style, fashion and the leisure class. While the practice of carrying the breed about in the inner recesses of garments died out in the 17th century in England, it would continue in France into the 18th century, and smallness continued to be esteemed just as much as before. Juvenile dogs were confined in small spaces to restrict growth until puberty and they were fed foods believed to stunt their growth.

Another trait that was prized nearly as much as petite size was coat. Naturally, gentleness of disposition and hygienic cleanliness were also highly valued and are mentioned in the expanded descriptions of the breed from the early years of the Enlightenment. Maltese did not drool or slobber much, were easy to housebreak and very tidy by nature. It was in the 18th century that the consistent type we recognize as the Maltese today was developed and recorded once and for all. A famous Reynolds portrait of the mid-18th century shows a Maltese looking very much as it does today. The breed is described in a late 18th century classification as the familiar dog

Their small size makes it easier to carry these dogs around and contributes greatly to their famed cuddliness.

It is hard for anyone not to fall in love with a Maltese. His characteristic long white hair and friendly disposition make him a sure winner.

of Malta and accorded the size of a squirrel with a long silky coat.

In France, the Maltese (also known as the Bichon), became quite rare for a time in the 18th century, though another ill-fated queen, Marie Antoinette, had one with her on the day of her beheading.

While the numbers of the breed would expand or shrink with trends and cycles, a certain core was maintained. This was fueled by active breeders as well as traders and merchants who supplied the whims and fancies of the nobility and the socially prominent. The market for the tiniest specimens of Maltese as lap-dog companions was ever-present.

Many names have been used to describe the Maltese over the years. In Tudor times it was called the comforter dog because he was used to suppress pain. It was believed that the dog's body heat would draw out pain, so the diminutive, lightweight dog was placed on painful areas of the body. Whether this practice had a purely placebo or psychological effect or the friendly, loving disposition of the Maltese was a distraction, it must have worked because it existed for hundreds of years.

Another name was the "shock dog," which referred to the appearance of the Maltese when its long coat wasn't properly tended and its untidy, unwashed appearance caused its hair to stand out in a shocking manner. He was called by others the little lion dog or Maltese lion dog

because of the custom in the late 18th and early 19th centuries of cutting the coat in such a way as to create the appearance of a lion with shaved legs and torso except for the ribs and a layer more of hair about the neck and back. This lion-trimmed Maltese, fashionable in the 18th century, should not be confused with the present day little lion dog, or Bichon Petit Chien Lion, a small cousin of the Maltese and rare breed found chiefly in France known as an offshoot of the Bichon Frise. This "modern" dog is a distinct regional rare breed, different from the Maltese in coat and size, and sharing only the hair styling common with the Maltese of centuries past.

Another relative mentioned earlier is the Bichon Frise, an ancient breed in its own right descended early on from the Maltese or an ancestor of the Maltese. The Bichon is a loosely curled, full bodied, coarser-coated dog than the Maltese (whose hair is straight, long and silky) and is larger in size, averaging two to three inches longer at the withers and having more spots on the coat. The Bichon and the little lion dog have coarse undercoats under their wavy, curly exterior coats.

Another descendant of the Maltese is the Havana Silk Dog, descended from Maltese brought by the Spaniards to the New World in the age of discovery (16th century). The breed, associated with Cuba (hence the name) and the West Indies, looks like the modern Maltese. He is a bigger dog and usually tan or light brown in color, rather than all white like the Maltese. The Bolognese is a close relative of the Maltese and descended from Maltese imported into Italy in the Middle Ages, then bred true in isolation. He closely resembles the Bichon Frise in size, color and configuration, but with a shorter, less curly coat.

The 19th century in England was a time of great interest in dog breeding for a variety of purposes. Dogs were bred for hunting, pest control, cruel dog fighting contests, work—especially shepherding, carriage companions, watch dogs—and, as always the case with the Maltese, as loving companions to the gentry. For a time the Maltese, as in other periods of ebb and flow,

became quite rare in Britain so that by the 1840s, they had all but disappeared. This changed with the interest of young Queen Victoria, who eventually acquired some Maltese imported from abroad. With the Queen's action came renewed interest in the breed. In the second decade of her reign, the leading dog authority of the day described the Maltese as weighing between 5 and 6.5 pounds. With his new-found popularity in Victorian England came the discovery that his fearless, feisty disposition made the Maltese an excellent rat killer and useful not just in pest control, but in the "sport" of ratting. This so-called sport put dogs, mostly terriers, in rings with large numbers of rats, which they were expected to kill in allotted

The Maltese's popularity skyrocketed in 19th century England. Here Ch. Titanic's Moppet's Boleroot Normalta is being offered a Victorian bath.

There was a proliferation of Maltese breeding activity in the late 19th century. Because they were considered status symbols many people wanted to own one of these beautiful animals.

time periods. Dogs with the most kills at the bell were declared winners while their owners, usually heavy betters, took home the prizes and winnings.

High-quality Maltese of the type kept by royalty remained rare. At one of the first dog shows in Britain, in 1862, twenty Maltese were exhibited. When the English Kennel Club was established in 1862, it registered 24 Maltese, and when it held its first show that same year there were Maltese competing against each other. There was a flurry of breeding activity and the Maltese's popularity increased in England between 1880 and 1910. Most of the English Maltese of this period were smaller than today's Maltese, a carry over from the old ideal of the lap dog of nobility. Three- and four-pound males and females were common. With the coming of the first World War interest in dog breeding fell off. The number of Maltese in Britain dropped off accordingly to the point that they became relatively rare. A standard was established for a Maltese dog other than white. It was smaller than the white with several color varieties allowed. The hair could be of a coarser texture and the heads

A hardy little animal, the Maltese is very adept at adjusting to different conditions. Here one demonstrates a zest for The Great Outdoors.

wider with shorter muzzles. These types or classifications appeared in English shows until 1913 when they, along with other canine activities, ceased abruptly with the onset of World War I.

While Maltese were present in the US in the 1870s, the great period of interest and importation occurred between 1910 and 1913, when the Maltese was most popular in Britain. In the late 19th century, both white and colored Maltese were shown at dog shows, especially the renowned Westminster Kennel Club show in New York, NY. In the 1880s and 90s, Maltese were shown in respectable numbers at major shows. The center of Maltese ownership and interest was largely New York City, where they were a fashion statement for the social set of this period. Despite this early start, and the increased breeding activity of the 1900-1913 period, the Maltese remained a rare breed whose numbers were limited all through the first half of this century. In 1950, there were only 73 Maltese

The popularity of the Maltese has grown tremendously among people of all ages. Today there are more Maltese alive in the world than have ever lived since their creation.

registered with the AKC. The second half of this century has seen an explosion of popularity that is astonishing. There are more Maltese alive in the world today than have ever lived back to the dawn of their creation. Today there is an American Maltese Association with more than 250 members. Happily, until quite recently, there had been no need for the association to organize a national breed rescue network, as few Maltese have been abandoned. This allowed the Association to devote most of its efforts to developing the highest standards of health and conformation for the breed. The first national Maltese dog club organized in the US was called the Maltese Terrier Club of America—the result of increased interest in the breed, both in Britain and the US, from 1890 through the early 1900s. As the name suggests, the club was based on the then common assumption that the Maltese was of terrier origin, a conception based, no doubt, on the Maltese's strong record in the ratting sport.

The club name was changed early on to the National Maltese Club (and later to the Maltese Dog Club of America). This club held the first local specialty show in New York and was able to produce a standard agreed upon and adapted by the American Kennel Club in 1906. This standard was heavily influenced and based largely on the British model established by the English Kennel Club with some American modifications.

By the 1950s, the Maltese Dog Club of America had a rival organization calling itself the Maltese Dog Fanciers of America. This group held a somewhat different view and philosophy of the standard than the older club.

Maltese ownership and breeding had by this time increased to the level that there was interest within both groups for a national specialty show. Application to the AKC for just such a sanctioned show was refused because of the division between the two clubs and a lack of consensus in establishing a sponsoring or parent club to sanction the show. This need plus dissatisfaction and disagreements within and between both clubs with the old 1906 standard produced a reconciliation and fusion of the two clubs in 1961. The result was the current American Maltese Association. This new club held national specialty shows in 1963 and 1964.

The Maltese enjoyed their first American specialty show in 1963. This is Ch. Reslos Lavis Riel being shown in New York in 1979.

One of the first orders of business of the now United Maltese Association was to modify and update the old 1906 standard. This was done accordingly in 1963 when a new standard was hammered out and accepted by the AKC. This standard eliminated the positive and negative point system and other parts of the old standard that were heavily based on the English model. Overall balanced quality was now more important than strict size, with the preferred size changing from under three pounds to from four to six pounds. The 1963 standard did not completely satisfy a fair percentage of the newly formed association. This was especially true of the 1963 standard lines describing head and muzzle. This standard was changed in 1964 by the association and approved by the AKC. The 1963 standard allows for a muzzle equal in length to the length of the skull, while the new 1964 standard described it as being merely of medium length. The 1964 standard has remained the standard for the breed and is the one in force today.

In the late 19th century, there was a great deal of interest in the colored Maltese, both in the US and abroad. In England, there were even two separate standards, with the white tolerating larger size. After WWI, interest in the colored Maltese waned. It is interesting to note that as with other breeds, the British standard

The American Kennel Club approves the standard for the Maltese written by the breed clubs. The standard descibes ideals for size, weight, and color.

Though originally shown in the Non-Sporting Group, the Maltese has found a permanent home in the Toy Group at AKC shows.

allowed for a weight of up to 12 pounds, reflecting the modern English taste for a larger dog. This is, of course, in stark contrast to the earlier aristocratic tiny dog of English society.

The current British standard calls for an all-white dog, to the exclusion of any other color. This was true of the American standard back to 1906, though later US standards allow for light tan or lemon spots on the ears, even though this is considered less desirable than all white. As noted, the American standard calls for a shorter or more moderate muzzle than the older English one.

Originally exhibited in the Miscellaneous Class, the Maltese was moved to show in the Non-Sporting Group before ending up in the Toy Group where it is

The Maltese pup is often mistaken for a spaniel or a terrier. However, there is no concrete evidence that suggests any relation with either of these.

shown today. The shifting from group to group is a reflection in part on the disagreement and debate at the end of the 19th century about the origins of the breed. First thought to be a terrier by some misinformed observers, the Maltese was later thought to be a spaniel in origin because of its body and coat type. The conventional wisdom of the first few decades of this century concluded that it was neither terrier nor spaniel, but was simply a "Maltese dog." Currently, new evidence has surfaced suggesting that the original Maltese was a spaniel-type dog and thus, by descent, the Maltese is a spaniel in origin, however changed over time. A description in a recent medical text describes the Maltese as "spaniel dogs, not terriers, that are usually spirited and healthy." The description goes on to read, "The adult Maltese tends to be extremely active, but his size precludes the necessity of large exercise areas. The average mature dog weighs five pounds. The breed is outgoing, inquisitive, friendly and often called the dog of a million kisses."

Thus we have the little Maltese, one of the oldest breeds known and probably the first to serve as a personal pet. The dog did not originate in Malta and probably began as a small spaniel-type dog in Central Europe that performed working duties. It was completely absent and unknown in Malta for large chunks of time (all through the Middle Ages down to the 19th century, when it was re-introduced). Its numbers have expanded and shrunk with the fashions and tastes of the times at various points and places in history.

Nevertheless, the Maltese has survived thousands of years and is thriving today. He is justly called the Maltese because it was there that he really became known to the civilized world. It was there that the Phoenicians, Greeks and Romans converted him into the little companion whose loving, yet snobbish appeal would last to this day. It was from Malta that, through trade and commerce, his value was established, his standard first put forward, and his fame spread far and wide. It is as a Maltese, therefore, that he is and will always be rightfully known.

The Maltese is sometimes referred to as "the dog of a million kisses." Here you can see why; note this pair's charm and inquisitiveness.

THE MALTESE STANDARD

The standard for the Maltese describes a toy dog with long, silky white hair. It calls for a single coat without undercoat that hangs long and flat and deep over the body of the animal, almost to the ground. His gait is described as a smooth, jaunty, flowing one with legs moving straight ahead. Any kind of movement to the sides or in and out is considered a serious fault. The coat, along with the described gait, should give the moving Maltese the impression of rapid movement. Temperament is described as fearless, trusting and affectionate. He is to be gentle, lively, playful and vigorous. His feet are to be small and round with black toe pads. The hind legs should be strong and only moderately angulated so that the stifles and hocks are not bent back to compensate.

The standard describes a toy dog under seven pounds—not the dwarf so favored in his aristocratic past. The modern Maltese is by definition a sound little dog, well put together for his size. Making allowance for size and weight, the Maltese is not frail, sickly or weak. The days of stunted growth are over. These dogs are usually spirited and healthy.

It is indisputable that the long, white, silky hair is probably the single most identifying mark of a show Maltese.

A Maltese without the long hair is almost a deadringer for a Bichon Frise. The puffed-up look is that which characterizes the Bichon.

This champion Maltese has the heavily feathered ears and dark round eyes called for in the standard.

The following is the Official Standard for the Maltese as adopted by the parent club and approved March 10, 1964:

General Appearance—The Maltese is a toy dog covered from head to foot with a mantle of long, silky, white hair. He is gentle-mannered and affectionate, eager and sprightly in action, and, despite his size, possesssed of the vigor needed for the satisfactory companion.

Head—Of medium length and in proportion to the size of the dog. The skull is slightly rounded on top, the stop moderate. The drop ears are rather low set and heavily feathered with long hair that hangs close to the head.

Eyes are set not too far apart; they are very dark and round, their black rims enhancing the gentle yet alert expression. The muzzle is of medium length, fine and tapered but not snipy. The nose is black. The teeth meet in an even, edge-to-edge bite, or in a scissors bite.

Neck—Sufficient length of neck is desirable as promoting a high carriage of the head.

Body—Compact, the height from the withers to the ground equaling the length from the withers to the root of the tail. Shoulder blades are sloping, the elbows well knit and held close to the body. The back is level in topline, the ribs well sprung. The chest is fairly deep, the loins taut, strong, and just slightly tucked up underneath.

Tail—A long-haired plume carried gracefully over the back, its tip lying to the side over the quarter.

Legs and Feet—Legs are fine-boned and nicely feathered. Forelegs are straight, their pastern joints well knit and devoid of appreciable bend. Hind legs are strong and moderately angulated at stifles and hocks. The feet are small and round, with toe pads black. Scraggly hairs on the feet may be trimmed to give a neater appearance.

Coat and Color—The coat is single, that is, without undercoat. It hangs long, flat and silky over the sides of the body almost, if not quite, to the ground. The long head-hair may be tied up in a topknot or it may be left hanging. Any suggestion of kinkiness, curliness, or woolly texture is objectionable. Color, pure white. Light tan or lemon on the ears is permissible, but not desirable.

Size—Weight under 7 pounds, with from 4 to 6 pounds preferred. Over-all quality is to be favored over size.

Gait—The Maltese moves with a jaunty, smooth, flowing gait. Viewed from the side, he gives an impression of rapid movement, size considered. In the stride, the forelegs reach straight and free from the shoulders, with elbows close. Hind legs to move in a stright line. Cowhocks or any suggestion of hind leg toeing in or out are faults.

Temperament—For all his diminutive size, the Maltese seems to be without fear. His trust and affectionate responsiveness are very appealing. He is among the gentlest mannered of all little dogs, yet he is lively and playful as well as vigorous.

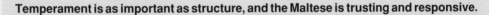
Temperament is as important as structure, and the Maltese is trusting and responsive.

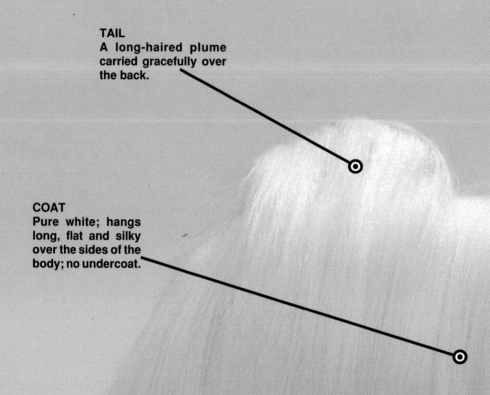

1996 Best of Breed Winner Ch. Merri Paloma owned by Barbara A. Merrick and David Fitzpatrick.

TAIL
A long-haired plume carried gracefully over the back.

COAT
Pure white; hangs long, flat and silky over the sides of the body; no undercoat.

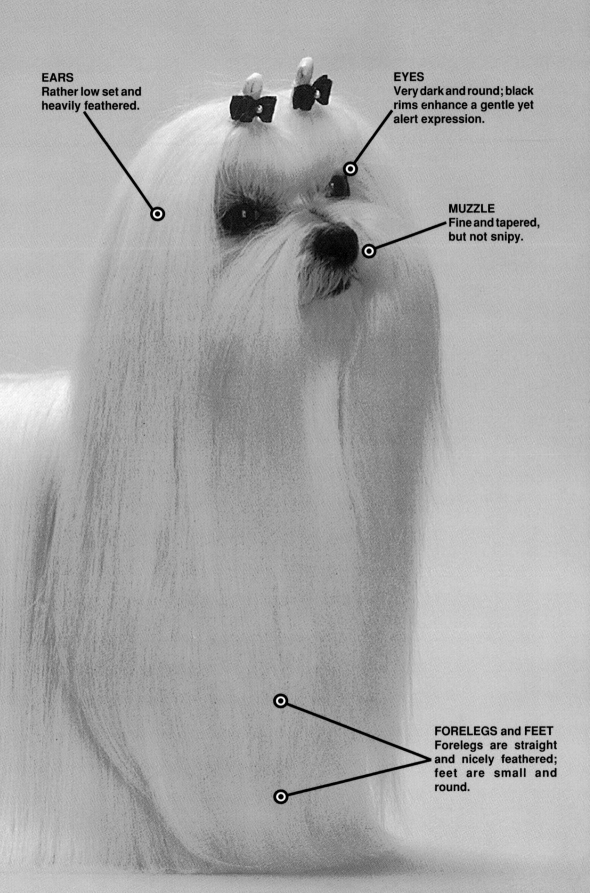

EARS
Rather low set and
heavily feathered.

EYES
Very dark and round; black
rims enhance a gentle yet
alert expression.

MUZZLE
Fine and tapered,
but not snipy.

FORELEGS and FEET
Forelegs are straight
and nicely feathered;
feet are small and
round.

YOUR NEW MALTESE PUPPY

SELECTION

When you do pick out a Maltese puppy as a pet, don't be hasty; the longer you study puppies, the better you will understand them. Make it your transcendent concern to select only one that radiates good health and spirit and is lively on his feet, whose eyes are bright, whose coat shines, and who comes forward eagerly to make and to cultivate your acquaintance. Don't fall for any shy little darling that wants to retreat to his bed or his box, or plays coy behind other puppies or people, or hides his head under your arm or jacket appealing to your protective instinct. *Pick the Maltese puppy who forthrightly picks you! The feeling of attraction should be mutual!*

DOCUMENTS

Now, a little paper work is in order. When you purchase a purebred Maltese puppy, you should receive a transfer of ownership, registration material, and other "papers" (a list of the immunization shots, if any, the puppy may have been given; a note on whether or not the puppy has been wormed; a diet and feeding schedule to which the puppy is accustomed) and you are

Maltese puppies are cute and irresistible. Choosing one is sometimes a difficult thing to do.

welcomed as a fellow owner to a long, pleasant association with a most lovable pet, and more (news)paper work.

GENERAL PREPARATION

You have chosen to own a particular Maltese puppy. You have chosen it very carefully over all other breeds and all other puppies. So before you ever get that Maltese puppy home, you will have prepared for its arrival by reading everything you can get your hands on having to do with the management of Malteses and puppies. True, you will run into many conflicting opinions, but at least you will not be starting "blind." Read, study, digest.

This newborn is learning an important lesson early—that gentle handling by people is enjoyable.

Talk over your plans with your veterinarian, other "Maltese people," and the seller of your Maltese puppy.

When you get your Maltese puppy, you will find that your reading and study are far from finished. You've just scratched the surface in your plan to provide the greatest possible comfort and health for your Maltese; and, by the same token, you do want to assure yourself of the greatest possible enjoyment of this wonderful creature. You must be ready for this puppy mentally as well as in the physical requirements.

TRANSPORTATION

If you take the puppy home by car, protect him from drafts, particularly in cold weather. Wrapped in a towel and carried in the arms or lap of a passenger, the Maltese puppy will usually make the trip without mishap. If the pup starts to drool and to squirm, stop the car for a few minutes. Have newspapers handy in case of car-sickness. A covered carton lined with newspapers provides protection for puppy and car, if you are driving alone. Avoid excitement and unnecessary handling of the puppy on arrival. A Maltese puppy is a very small "package" to be making a complete change of surroundings and company, and he needs frequent rest and refreshment to renew his vitality.

It is not a good idea to bring home a pet during the holiday season. The increased excitement only frightens the animal, and can slow down the process of acclimating to the new surroundings.

THE FIRST DAY AND NIGHT

When your Maltese puppy arrives in your home, put him down on the floor and don't pick him up again, except when it is absolutely necessary. He is a dog, a real dog, and must not be lugged around like a rag doll. Handle him as little as possible, and permit no one to pick him up and baby him. To repeat, *put your Maltese puppy on the floor or the ground and let him stay there except when it may be necessary to do otherwise.*

Quite possibly your Maltese puppy will be afraid for a while in his new surroundings, without his mother and littermates. Comfort him and reassure him, but don't console him. Don't give him the "oh-you-poor-itsy-bitsy-puppy" treatment. Be calm, friendly, and reassuring. Encourage him to walk around and sniff over his new home. If it's dark, put on the lights. Let him roam for a few minutes while you and everyone else concerned sit quietly or go about your routine business. Let the puppy come back to you.

Playmates may cause an immediate problem if the new Maltese puppy is to be greeted by children or other pets. If not, you can skip this subject. The natural affinity between puppies and children calls for some supervision until a live-and-let-live relationship is established. This applies particularly to a Christmas puppy, when there is more excitement than usual and more chance for a puppy to swallow something upsetting. It is a better plan to welcome the puppy several days before or after the holiday week. Like a baby, your Maltese puppy needs much rest and should not be over-handled. Once a child realizes that a puppy has "feelings" similar to his own, and can readily be hurt or injured, the opportunities for play and responsibilities provide exercise and training for both.

For his first night with you, he should be put where he is to sleep every night—say in the kitchen, since its floor can usually be easily cleaned. Let him explore the kitchen to his heart's content; close doors to confine him there. Prepare his food and feed him lightly the first night. Give him a pan with some water in it—not a lot, since most puppies will try to drink the whole pan dry. Give him

As with a baby, your Maltese puppy needs a lot of rest and should not be overhandled.

an old coat or shirt to lie on. Since a coat or shirt will be strong in human scent, he will pick it out to lie on, thus furthering his feeling of security in the room where he has just been fed.

HOUSEBREAKING HELPS

Now, sooner or later—mostly sooner—your new Maltese puppy is going to "puddle" on the floor. First take a newspaper and lay it on the puddle until the urine is soaked up onto the paper. *Save this paper.* Now take a cloth with soap and water, wipe up the floor and dry it well. Then take the wet paper and place it on a fairly large square of newspapers in a convenient corner. When cleaning up, always keep a piece of wet paper on top of the others. Every time he wants to "squat," he will seek out this spot and use the papers. (This routine is rarely necessary for more than three days.) Now leave your Maltese puppy for the night. Quite probably he will cry and howl a bit; some are more stubborn than others on this matter. But let him stay alone for the night. This may seem harsh treatment, but it is the best procedure in the long run. Just let him cry; he will weary of it sooner or later.

FEEDING

Now let's talk about feeding your Maltese, a subject so simple that it's amazing there is so much nonsense and misunderstanding about it. Is it expensive to feed a Maltese? No, it is not! You can feed your Maltese economically and keep him in perfect shape the year round, or you can feed him expensively. He'll thrive either way, and let's see why this is true.

First of all, remember a Maltese is a dog. Dogs do not have a high degree of selectivity in their food, and unless you spoil them with great variety (and possibly turn them into poor, "picky" eaters) they will eat almost anything that they become accustomed to. Many dogs flatly refuse to eat nice, fresh beef. They pick around it and eat everything else. But meat—bah! Why? They aren't accustomed to it! They'd eat rabbit fast enough, but they refuse beef because they aren't used to it.

It is best to feed your Maltese puppy the same food he was eating before you brought him home. Any change in diet should be made gradually.

VARIETY NOT NECESSARY

A good general rule of thumb is forget all human preferences and don't give a thought to variety. Choose the right diet for your Maltese and feed it to him day after day, year after year, winter and summer. But what is the right diet?

Hundreds of thousands of dollars have been spent in canine nutrition research. The results are pretty conclusive, so you needn't go into a lot of experimenting with trials of this and that every other week. Research has proven just what your dog needs to eat and to keep healthy.

DOG FOOD

There are almost as many right diets as there are dog experts, but the basic diet most often recommended is one that consists of a dry food, either meal or kibble form. There are several of excellent quality, manufactured by reliable companies, research tested, and nationally advertised. They are inexpensive, highly satisfactory, and easily available in stores everywhere in containers of five to 50 pounds. Larger amounts cost less per pound, usually.

If you have a choice of brands, it is usually safer to choose the

Maltese are usually not very selective eaters, unless you make them so. Feed the dog what is good for him and forget about human dietary preferences.

When the puppies get used to their diet, they will clamor all over themselves at feeding time to get to the bowl.

moist or canned types of dog foods, if you decide to feed one of these.

Having chosen a really good food, feed it to your Maltese as the manufacturer directs. And once you've started, stick to it. Never change if you can possibly help it. A switch from one meal or kibble-type food can usually be made without too much upset; however, a change will almost invariably give you (and your Maltese) some trouble.

better known one; but even so, carefully read the analysis on the package. Do not choose any food in which the protein level is less than 25 percent, and be sure that this protein comes from both animal and vegetable sources. The good dog foods have meat meal, fish meal, liver, and such, plus protein from alfalfa and soy beans, as well as some dried-milk product. Note the vitamin content carefully. See that they are all there in good proportions; and be especially certain that the food contains properly high levels of vitamins A and D, two of the most perishable and important ones. Note the B-complex level, but don't worry about carbohydrate and mineral levels. These substances are plentiful and cheap and not likely to be lacking in a good brand.

The advice given for how to choose a dry food also applies to

WHEN SUPPLEMENTS ARE NEEDED

Now what about supplements of various kinds, mineral and vitamin, or the various oils? They are all okay to add to your Maltese's food. However, if you are feeding your Maltese a correct diet, and this is easy to do, no supplements are necessary unless your Maltese has been improperly fed, has been sick, or is having puppies. Vitamins and minerals are naturally present in all the foods; and to ensure against any loss through processing, they are added in concentrated form to the dog food you use. Except on the advice of your veterinarian, added amounts of vitamins can prove harmful to your Maltese! The same risk goes with minerals.

FEEDING SCHEDULE

When and how much food to give your Maltese? Most dogs do better if fed two or three smaller meals per day—this is not only better but vital to larger and deep-chested dogs. As to how to prepare the food and how much to give, it is generally best to follow the directions on the food package. Your own Maltese may want a little more or a little less.

Fresh, cool water should always be available to your Maltese. This is important to good health throughout his lifetime.

ALL MALTESE NEED TO CHEW

Puppies and young Maltese need something with resistance to chew on while their teeth and jaws are developing—for cutting the puppy teeth, to induce growth of the permanent teeth under the puppy teeth, to assist in getting

There are special bones made just for puppies. They usually contain calcium supplements and are very hard. The most popular of the puppy bones is the one made by Nylabone®.

rid of the puppy teeth at the proper time, to help the permanent teeth through the gums, to ensure normal jaw development, and to settle the permanent teeth solidly in the jaws.

The adult Maltese's desire to chew stems from the instinct for tooth cleaning, gum massage, and jaw exercise—plus the need for an outlet for periodic doggie tensions.

This is why dogs, especially puppies and young dogs, will often destroy property worth hundreds of dollars when their chewing instinct is not diverted from their owner's possessions. And this is why you should provide your Maltese with something to chew—something that has the necessary functional qualities, is desirable from the Maltese's viewpoint, and is safe for him.

It is very important that your Maltese not be permitted to chew on anything he can break or on any indigestible thing from which he can bite sizable chunks. Sharp pieces, such as from a bone which can be broken by a dog, may pierce the intestinal wall and kill. Indigestible things that can be bitten off in chunks, such as from shoes or rubber or plastic toys, may cause an intestinal stoppage (if not regurgitated) and bring painful death, unless surgery is promptly performed.

Strong natural bones, such as 4- to 8-inch lengths of round shin bone from mature beef—either the kind you can get from a butcher or one of the variety available commercially in pet stores—may serve your Maltese's teething needs if his mouth is large enough to handle them effectively. You may be tempted to give your Maltese puppy a smaller bone and he may not be able to break it when you do, but puppies grow rapidly and the power of their jaws constantly increases until maturity. This means that a growing Maltese may break one of the smaller bones at any time, swallow the pieces, and die painfully before you realize what is wrong.

All hard natural bones are very abrasive. If your Maltese is an avid chewer, natural bones may wear away his teeth prematurely; hence, they then should be taken away from your dog when the teething purposes have been served. The badly worn, and usually painful, teeth of many mature dogs can be traced to excessive chewing on natural bones.

Contrary to popular belief, knuckle bones that can be chewed up and swallowed by your Maltese provide little, if any, usable calcium or other nutriment. They do, however, disturb the digestion of most dogs and cause them to vomit the nourishing food they need.

Dried rawhide products of various types, shapes, sizes, and prices are available on the market and have become quite popular. However, they don't serve the primary chewing functions very well; they are a bit messy when wet from mouthing, and most Maltese chew them up rather rapidly—but they have been considered safe for dogs until recently. Now, more and more incidents of death, and near death, by strangulation have been reported to be the results of partially swallowed chunks of rawhide swelling in the throat. More recently, some veterinarians

Molded rawhide, called Roarhide® by Nylabone®, is very hard and very safe for your dog. It is eagerly accepted by Maltese.

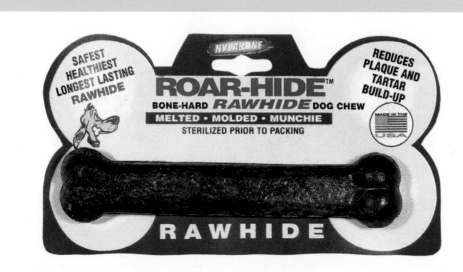

Most Nylabone® products—like the Carrot Bone™—provide the necessary resistance to facilitate good jaw exercise in the dog.

have been attributing cases of acute constipation to large pieces of incompletely digested rawhide in the intestine.

A new product, molded rawhide, is very safe. During the process, the rawhide is melted and then injection molded into the familiar dog shape. It is very hard and is eagerly accepted by Maltese. The melting process also sterilizes the rawhide. Don't confuse this with pressed rawhide, which is nothing more than small strips of rawhide squeezed together.

The nylon bones, especially those with natural meat and bone fractions added, are probably the most complete, safe, and economical answer to the chewing need. Dogs cannot break them or bite off sizable chunks; hence,

they are completely safe—and being longer lasting than other things offered for the purpose, they are economical.

Hard chewing raises little bristle-like projections on the surface of the nylon bones—to provide effective interim tooth cleaning and vigorous gum massage, much in the same way your toothbrush does it for you. The little projections are raked off and swallowed in the form of thin shavings, but the chemistry of the nylon is such that they break down in the stomach fluids and pass through without effect.

The toughness of the nylon provides the strong chewing resistance needed for important jaw exercise and effectively aids teething functions, but there is no tooth wear because nylon is non-

Periodic dental checkups are necessary for your Maltese even if you provide superior chews such as Nylabone® and Gumabone® products.

abrasive. Being inert, nylon does not support the growth of microorganisms; and it can be washed in soap and water or it can be sterilized by boiling or in an autoclave.

Nylabone® is highly recommended by veterinarians as a safe, healthy nylon bone that can't splinter or chip. Nylabone® is frizzled by the dog's chewing action, creating a toothbrush-like surface that cleanses the teeth and massages the gums. Nylabone®, the only chew products made of flavor-impregnated solid nylon, are available in your local pet shop. Nylabone® is superior to the cheaper bones because it is made of virgin nylon, which is the strongest and longest-lasting type of nylon available. The cheaper bones are made from recycled or re-ground nylon scraps, and have a tendency to break apart and split easily.

Nothing, however, substitutes for periodic professional attention for your Maltese's teeth and gums, not any more than your toothbrush can do that for you. Have your Maltese's teeth cleaned at least once a year by your veterinarian (twice a year is better) and he will be happier, healthier, and far more pleasant to live with.

TRAINING

You owe proper training to your Maltese. The right and privilege of being trained is his birthright; and whether your Maltese is going to be a handsome, well-mannered housedog and companion, a show dog, or whatever possible use he may be put to, the basic training is always the same—all must start with basic obedience, or what might be called "manner training."

Your Maltese must come instantly when called and obey the "Sit" or "Down" command just as fast; he must walk quietly at "Heel," whether on or off lead. He must be mannerly and polite wherever he goes; he must be polite to strangers on the street and in stores. He must be mannerly in the presence of other dogs. He must not bark at

Whether you have a puppy or an adult, it's a good idea to train your Maltese to be a well-behaved companion.

As soon as possible, get the puppy comfortable with chewing on a poly bone. This will be invaluable in maintaining good teeth in the long run.

children on roller skates, motorcycles, or other domestic animals. And he must be restrained from chasing cats. It is not a dog's inalienable right to chase cats, and he must be reprimanded for it.

a "good dog." If you enlist the services of a good professional trainer, follow his advice of when to come to see the dog. No, he won't forget you, but too-frequent visits at the wrong time may slow down his training progress. And

Don't let your Maltese puppy do things that will not be tolerated when he's an adult, such as sitting on the furniture. Be consistent in your training and the results will be a well-mannered dog.

PROFESSIONAL TRAINING

How do you go about this training? Well, it's a very simple procedure, pretty well standardized by now. First, if you can afford the extra expense, you may send your Maltese to a professional trainer, where in 30 to 60 days he will learn how to be

using a "pro" trainer means that you will have to go for some training, too, after the trainer feels your Maltese is ready to go home. You will have to learn how your Maltese works, just what to expect of him and how to use what the dog has learned after he is home.

OBEDIENCE TRAINING CLASS

Another way to train your Maltese (many experienced Maltese people think this is the best) is to join an obedience training class right in your own community. There is such a group in nearly every community nowadays. Here you will be working with a group of people who are also just starting out. You will actually be training your own dog, since all work is done under the direction of a head trainer who will make suggestions to you and also tell you when and how to correct your Maltese's errors. Then, too, working with such a group, your Maltese will learn to get along with other dogs. And, what is more important, he will learn to do exactly what he is told to do, no matter how much confusion there is around him or how great the temptation is to go his own way.

You should also train your Maltese to respond well to wire crates and cages. These are necessary for transportation and housebreaking.

Write to your national kennel club for the location of a training club or class in your locality. Sign up. Go to it regularly—every session! Go early and leave late! Both you and your Maltese will benefit tremendously.

TRAIN HIM BY THE BOOK

The third way of training your Maltese is by the book. Yes, you can do it this way and do a good job of it too. But in using the book method, select a book, buy it, study it carefully; then study it some more, until the procedures are almost second nature to you. Then start your training. But stay with the book and its advice and exercises. Don't start in and then make up a few rules of your own. If you don't follow the book, you'll get into jams you can't get out of by yourself. If after a few hours of short training sessions your Maltese is still not working as he should, get back to the book for a study session, because it's your fault, not the dog's! The procedures of dog training have been so well systemized that it must be your fault, since literally thousands of fine Malteses have been trained by the book.

After your Maltese is "letter perfect" under all conditions, then, if you wish, go on to advanced training and trick work.

Your Maltese will love his obedience training, and you'll burst with pride at the finished product! Your Maltese will enjoy life even more, and you'll enjoy your Maltese more. And remember—you *owe good training to your Maltese.*

GROOMING

More than anything else, the Maltese has been called by many dog fanciers a head and coat breed. Great emphasis is given in the standard to coat, which is described as long, white and silky. This coat can become filthy if not kept clean, as the aristocracy of old discovered to their chagrin while keeping Maltese in their sleeves. This trait probably accounts for the abandonment of the practice.

The actual quality or silkiness of the coat is more important than the sheer quantity. Rough- and course-textured coats are considered undesirable. While coat texture is largely genetically determined, the standard does not permit any cutting or trimming of the main body of hair, only to the feet and back of hocks. Some trimming may be necessary if the coat, which can reach to the floor, inhibits the dog's comfort. If the Maltese is not being shown, a slightly shorter cut can be given; but even for show purposes, excessive length should be trimmed. While there is no such thing as a show cut, the Maltese needs to be shampooed and combed regularly. There are a

The appearance of the coat is an integral part of a show Maltese's features. Much care should be taken to keep the coat well-groomed and mat free.

Shampooing your Maltese is highly desirable because of the excessive length of the hair. However, make sure that the correct shampoo is used otherwise overdrying or flaking of the skin may develop.

variety of hair products available to assist nature and the groomer.

Shampooing with a product with the correct pH balance is a must. There are special dog shampoos suitable for a Maltese; ask for a recommendation from your veterinarian or a reputable breeder. The hair of a Maltese is different from most other breeds, and shampoos that are suitable for those breeds may not be right for your Maltese. Shampoos for humans will be unsuitable. Maltese can be shampooed frequently as needed. Trial and error will determine how often the coat can safely be washed without the skin drying out or flaking. Good conditioners are a must, as are other useful products that can help maintain the proper balance of oil and moisture in the hair. Again, conditioners exist for different conditions and a dog-to-dog trial approach as well as good professional advice is in order.

Frequent brushing several times a week is usually necessary. The delicate nature of the Maltese coat requires that the brushing be done carefully so as not to rip and break the coat. Natural bristle brushes, not nylon or other man-made products, should be used. Grooming must be done properly and mistakes can be costly. Owners new to the breed should consider having their dogs groomed professionally when preparing for shows.

The great length of the Maltese coat increases the potential for matting. Certain parts of the coat are more prone to matting than others, such as the rear areas and behind the ears. There is individual variance from dog to dog in the frequency and the extent of matting. However fast the coat mats, it must be brushed and combed out immediately and done carefully and skillfully. A harsh brushing action or extensive pulling can rip up patches of coat and spoil the dog's appearance. All combs used should be the special steel canine combing type made especially for this purpose. They are sold in pet supply stores and at dog shows. Like brushing and bathing, the novice should seek professional advice about combing, including which size comb to use. Drying the Maltese can also be a project. Many exhibitors, breeders and owners use blow-dry machines

A daily brushing with a short-bristle brush will keep your Maltese's coat looking nice and healthy.

exclusively to dry the long Maltese coat after bathing and shampooing. Serious Maltese exhibitors go to great lengths to condition the coat before shows, including using oils, waxes and hot, damp towels very much like those used in old-fashioned barber shops. While this may seem a bit extreme to many dog owners and even Maltese people, the results can be striking.

Properly groomed, the hair of the Maltese is parted directly down the center of the dog, so that the coat lies symmetrically flat and even on both sides. Eventually the part will become partially trained, making it easier to comb. The Maltese is one of the few breeds that has a permanently parted coat, and the parting is a very important and delicate matter and very essential to good coat management.

Many Maltese owners recoil at the thought of making so much fuss over their pet's coat. The time, expense and labor involved can be burdensome. Many pet Maltese have a less than perfect coat which can be somewhat coarser textured than the ideal and which no amount of fuss and bother can straighten out or make softer. Others with beautiful coats can be maintained with a less ambitious program of shampooing, bathing, brushing and combing, still resulting in a

Part the hair down the middle of the back and comb from the skin outward to get the maximum effect.

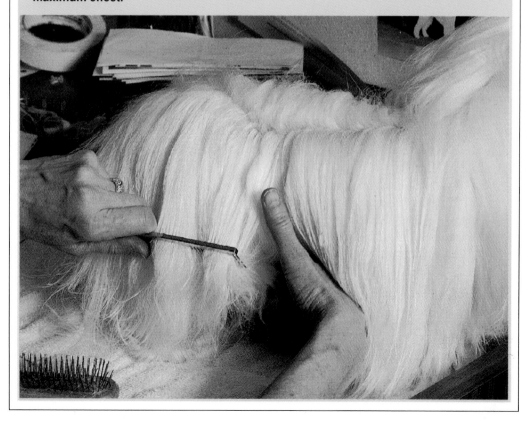

Be firm yet gentle when brushing the animal's coat. You do not want to inflict pain on your Maltese by roughly plowing through his matted hair.

healthy, attractive look, if somewhat less spectacular and dramatic than show presentation. Many owners will elect to gently towel dry their pets, the technique used for ages before the invention of the blow dryer.

Whatever techniques are elected, all Maltese should be kept clean, free from mats and decently brushed out as a matter of good canine hygiene and dog comfort. A prospective Maltese owner should be prepared to render this minimum standard.

In the final analysis, coat quality is a product of three basic factors. The first and foremost is genetic. No amount of grooming can make a beautiful coat on a dog that doesn't have the right genetic propensity. There are throwbacks to early models of Maltese that were coarse coated, colored, and other traits now considered off standard. Hair texture, strength and beauty are very much inherited characteristics. If the dog doesn't have it in him, he won't produce a beautiful coat no matter what you do. You can only assist nature, not make it.

The second basic factor is nutrition, and this is one you can assist with. A sound diet with a well-balanced program of

If a Maltese does not have good genetic makeup, no amount of grooming and primping will make a big difference to his looks.

Most Maltese are well-behaved when being groomed, as they enjoy the one-on-one attention. This dog is getting his hair wrapped to protect it from breaking.

nutritional supplements will go a long way toward assisting a grooming regimen. Puppies should be fed three times a day and adult dogs twice. Some Maltese may experience allergic reactions to certain foods and commercial preparations, and this may manifest itself in poor coat because of itchy, scaly skin or just plain poor growth and texture. Again, professional advice from a reputable breeder or exhibitor or a veterinarian interested in nutrition can be very useful and is recommended. There are tests to measure allergies if they are suspected.

Even if there are no allergies present, certain dogs will react better to certain foods, again suggesting a dog-by-dog approach and a bit of trial and error. All changes in diet must be gradual and the Maltese should be weaned from one food to the other carefully.

The third and final factor, and the subject of this section, is grooming. If the other factors are positive, grooming can make all the difference. You must have good genes and provide sound, balanced nutrition if your grooming efforts, however Herculean, are to pay off.

Proper grooming starts at an early age. This puppy admires his well-coiffed Mom.

SHOWING YOUR MALTESE

A show Maltese is a comparatively rare thing. He is one out of several litters of puppies. He happens to be born with a degree of physical perfection that closely automatically command a high price for service.

Showing Malteses is a lot of fun—yes, but it is a highly competitive sport. While all the experts were once beginners, the

Most Maltese are born conforming to the standard by which they are judged. However, their natural magnificence must be accentuated by proper care.

approximates the standard by which the breed is judged in the show ring. Such a dog should, on maturity, be able to win or approach his championship in good, fast company at the larger shows. Upon finishing his championship, he is apt to be as highly desirable as a breeding animal. As a proven stud, he will odds are against a novice. You will be showing against experienced handlers, often people who have devoted a lifetime to breeding, picking the right ones, and then showing those dogs through to their championships. Moreover, the most perfect Maltese ever born has faults, and in your hands

The key to success is adhering strictly to the standards by which the Maltese is judged. Ch. Sale's Screech Owl, bred by Barbara Bergquist, owned by B.B. Kathy DiGiacomo and Jeni Walters, is a prime example of a championship dog.

the faults will be far more evident than with the experienced handler who knows how to minimize his Maltese's faults. These are but a few points on the sad side of the picture.

The experienced handler, as I say, was not born knowing the ropes. He learned—*and so can you!* You can if you will put in the same time, study and keen observation that he did. But it will take time!

KEY TO SUCCESS

First, search for a truly fine show prospect. Take the puppy home, raise him by the book, and as carefully as you know how, give him every chance to mature into the Maltese you hoped for. My advice is to keep your dog out of big shows, even Puppy Classes, until he is mature. Maturity in the male is roughly two years; with the female, 14 months or so. When your Maltese is approaching maturity, start out at match shows, and, with this experience for both of you, then go gunning for the big wins at the big shows.

Next step, read the standard by which the Maltese is judged. Study it until you know it by heart. Having done this, and while your puppy is at home (where he should be) growing into a normal, healthy Maltese, go to every dog show you can possibly reach. Sit at the ringside and watch Maltese judging. Keep your ears and eyes open. Do your own judging, holding each of those dogs against the standard, which you now know by heart.

In your evaluations, don't start looking for faults. Look for the virtues—the best qualities. How does a given Maltese shape up against the standard? Having looked for and noted the virtues, then note the faults and see what prevents a given Maltese from standing correctly or moving well. Weigh these faults against the virtues, since, ideally, every feature of the dog should contribute to the harmonious whole dog.

The entire family can share in the joys of your Maltese winning a competition. Here Ch. Kathan's Tangerine poses for a picture with members of his family.

The Maltese's even temperament and flowing white coat give him an air of distinction in the show ring.

"RINGSIDE JUDGING"

It's a good practice to make notes on each Maltese, always holding the dog against the standard. In "ringside judging," forget your personal preference for this or that feature. What does the standard say about it? Watch carefully as the judge places the dogs in a given class. It is difficult from the ringside always to see why number one was placed over the second dog. Try to follow the judge's reasoning. Later try to talk with the judge after he is finished. Ask him questions as to why he placed certain Malteses and not others. Listen while the judge explains his placings, and, I'll say right here, any judge worthy of his license should be able to give reasons.

When you're not at the ringside, talk with the fanciers and breeders who have Malteses. Don't be afraid to ask opinions or say that you don't know. You have a lot of listening to do, and it will help you a great deal and speed up your personal progress if you are a good listener.

THE NATIONAL CLUB

You will find it worthwhile to join the national Maltese club and to subscribe to its magazine. From the national club, you will learn the location of an approved regional club near you. Now, when your young Maltese is eight to ten months old, find out the dates of match shows in your section of the country. These differ from regular shows only in that no championship points are given. These shows are especially designed to launch young dogs (and new handlers) on a show career.

ENTER MATCH SHOWS

With the ring deportment you have watched at big shows firmly in mind and practice, enter your Maltese in as many match shows as you can. When in the ring, you have two jobs. One is to see to it that your Maltese is always being seen to its best advantage. The other job is to keep your eye on the judge to see what he may want you to do next. Watch only the judge and your Maltese. Be quick and be alert; do exactly as the judge directs. Don't speak to him except to answer his questions. If he does something you don't like, don't say so. And don't irritate the judge (and everybody else) by constantly talking and fussing with your dog.

In moving about the ring, remember to keep clear of dogs beside you or in front of you. It is my advice to you *not* to show your Maltese in a regular point show until he is at least close to maturity and after both you and your dog have had time to perfect ring manners and poise in the match shows.

What constitutes a good show dog? One that has good poise and good "ring manners."

A healthy and happy Maltese will fit into any environment.

YOUR HEALTHY MALTESE

The Maltese would not have survived all these centuries if he wasn't a hardy little fellow, despite his somewhat delicate appearance. Nevertheless, there are some medical problems typical of, or more common to, the Maltese than some other breeds. One such problem is difficulty with delivery (whelping), especially in the first whelp or delivery for the dog. A female should be watched closely as the time for whelping approaches. The assistance of a veterinarian is frequently required during delivery; Caesarean births are rare but not unknown with the Maltese. It is wise to cut back the coat of the pregnant female well in advance of delivery.

There are several disorders or birth defects that affect the Maltese puppy. There is a fairly high incidence of hypoglycemia in the Maltese. This condition is only a problem in puppyhood and is outgrown as the Maltese reaches adulthood. It occurs when the concentration of glucose in the blood stream falls below the normal limit, in other words, low blood sugar. A sudden and dramatic drop in the blood sugar of a Maltese pup can induce shock, and in some cases, if not recognized and treated, the Maltese can grow weak and collapse. In rare cases, fatalities occur. Such an extreme reaction is usually hereditary and more likely to occur in certain bloodlines and breedings. The condition and its symptoms should be recognized early for safety sake. The signs are wobbliness, excessive drooling, pale gums and behavioral

Like humans, dogs are not immune from risky births. A healthy litter is sometimes prey to various illnesses such as hypoglycemia, which is common in the Maltese breed.

abnormalities. Honey or other high-fructose products such as corn syrup should be administered at the first sign of an attack. Your veterinarian can recommend other measures that can be taken to prevent or reduce the severity of hypoglycemic incidents in the Maltese puppy. There are glucose tolerance tests that a vet can use to determine whether or not the condition is present in your pet. With proper precaution, the affected dog will mature out of danger and be free

No one can deny that the Maltese's charm and good looks add to its constant appeal.

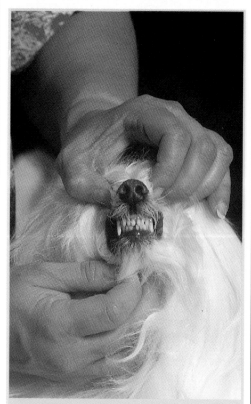

The teeth should be checked for any signs of double dentition (an extra set of teeth which must be extracted).

Double dentition or the presence of extra teeth in the mouth occurs when the puppy teeth fail to fall out of the maturing Maltese's mouth. These retained extra teeth must be extracted.

There is a degree of monorchidism or the presence of only one testicle in the scrotum in some male puppies at birth. This condition can cause problems if the retained testicle does not fall into place naturally during maturation or is removed by surgical neutering and/or removal of the retained testicle. Dogs with this defect in their bloodlines should not be bred.

A good, healthy puppy will exhibit controlled behavior even when being groomed, and will not have to be restrained.

of the abnormality by the age of one. Multiple feedings—even more than the three recommended per day for puppies—may well be prescribed by the vet.

A more serious birth defect found in some Maltese bloodlines is hydrocephalus, or water on the brain. This is caused by extra or excess fluid on the brain and sometimes occurs in the newborn. Rarely are steps taken to save these newborn pups. This severe birth defect has to be treated with a drain tube to relieve pressure on the swollen head by draining the fluid to the spinal cord or into a major blood vessel, a procedure almost unheard of in dogs.

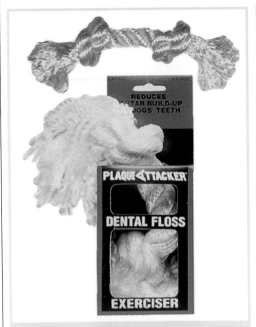

Nylafloss® serves two major purposes: it provides good exercise for the dog and helps in removing destructive plaque from beneath the gumline.

caution in harmony with sound genetics is employed. The very size of the gene pool and the incidence of line breeding are themselves a potential for some aberrations.

Sadly there is some deafness and congenital blindness in some bloodlines and the potential Maltese buyer should carefully investigate as best as possible the genetic ancestry of his new pup. Buying from a reputable and

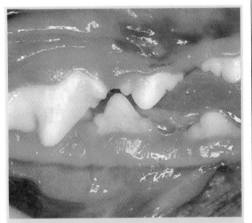

A scientific study shows how a dog's tooth can remain tartar free while being maintained by Gumabone® chewing.

Without the Gumabone® the tooth will be completely covered in plaque and tartar after about 30 days.

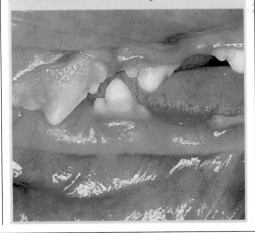

Another birth defect that can be treated successfully with surgery is patellar luxation, a defect of the knee caps which can cause lameness at four to six months of age. In this condition the knee caps curve in abnormally and tend to pop in and out, causing dislocations. The condition may or may not require surgery, and as with other defects, affected animals should not be bred.

Aberrant cilia or abnormal hair growth, especially when it takes the form of eyelashes that rub against the eyes, is one irregularity sometimes found in Maltese. This is never serious and not a consideration in breeding. Large-scale breeding to meet the increased demand for Maltese has inevitable consequences. This is true even when reasonable conscientious breeder will go a long way toward securing a healthy puppy free of birth defects.

The American Maltese Association, which has never felt the need for a rescue service in the past, is now organizing one. The Association also provides advisories to prospective purchasers, which include information about grooming and health-related matters. It is a good source for those who are searching for a reputable breeder. The association publishes a bulletin available to non-members for a $25 annual fee. It deals with all matters regarding the Maltese, including health and grooming.

The Maltese for all his feisty and fearless disposition, is still a toy breed somewhat frail in the sense that he is so small and light. As he doesn't need much space, he can make an ideal companion for apartment dwellers. This is especially true because he sheds very little hair and can be trained to keep barking to a minimum. This, plus the fact that he is tidy and clean by nature, may make him irresistible to some families with little living space. It is always important, though, to remember the Maltese's delicate traits and to realize that households with small children who are rough or difficult to control or who lack the

Because Maltese don't take up much space, they are ideal for apartment dwellers.

The Maltese is indisputably one of the most affectionate of dogs, and that is one of the reasons why it has remained in the public's favor for so many years.

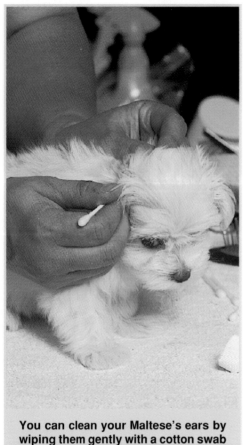

You can clean your Maltese's ears by wiping them gently with a cotton swab dipped in hydrogen peroxide.

he lives in a tick-infested area he should be inoculated against Lyme disease. The Maltese puppy's stool should be examined carefully for signs of worms and the puppy should be wormed whenever necessary to ensure proper health and growth.

As with all dogs, regular examination by a veterinarian at designated intervals is a necessity. All in all, despite these recited potential defects, the Maltese is, by and large, a sound little dog free of many of the maladies such as hip dysplasia that affect other larger and popular breeds.

The Maltese has managed to persevere and survive for most, if not all, of man's known history. He has survived periods of near

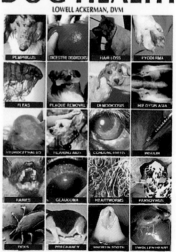

maturity and sensitivity to deal with the Maltese should not have one. Many breeders will not sell or place a Maltese in such a situation.

As with all pets with long hair, it is especially important to keep the Maltese parasite-free. The Maltese should have all regular shots, including parvo, distemper, rabies and every shot recommended by your vet to meet local conditions. Maltese in warm climates where there is a mosquito population should be kept on a heartworm medication regimen. While the Maltese is seldom a roaming or yard dog, if

If you take care of your Maltese he will reward you with many years of love and loyalty.

He has endured so well that at the end of 1995 there were 16,179 Maltese registered with the American Kennel Club and he ranked in 21st place overall in all-breed registrations. Forty-five years earlier, in 1950, there were only 73 Maltese registered. This rise would be remarkable if it involved a new or little-known breed; in fact, its taking place with an ancient breed enjoying a renaissance or new golden age is absolutely incredible.

The Maltese has served as a fashion statement for the affluent for many years. Terms such as "the little white dog of antiquity" and "the dog of a million kisses" will undoubtedly be used to describe this handsome animal for a long time.

extinction with the changes of taste and fashion and the distractions of wars, mass migrations, fallen empires, the ages of darkness and the Enlightenment. He has been bred down to a size so tiny as to be an ornament of dress and a portable bauble for the high born and he has chased and killed rats in rings for the sport and amusement of the lower orders. He is called the Maltese even though there were no Maltese in Malta for over a thousand years and some of his varieties, such as the colored Maltese, have all but disappeared.

SUGGESTED READING

OTHER T.F.H. BOOKS ON THE MALTESE

THE BOOK OF THE MALTESE
H-1067

The Book Of The Maltese is the largest and most comprehensive book available about the breed. Written by Joan McDonald Brearley and illustrated with over 100 full-color photos, this book covers an extensive number of topics—everything from breed history, breed champions, feeding, grooming, and proper care. The popular Maltese is brought to life in all 288 pages of this exciting volume and it is a must-have for any person who owns, cares for, or admires the Maltese.

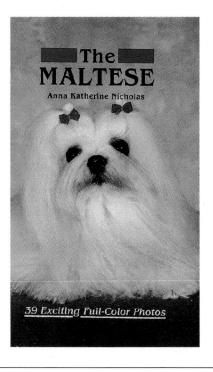

THE MALTESE
PS-803

Written by longtime breed expert Anna Katherine Nicholas, *The Maltese* is illustrated with over 150 full-color photos and covers all aspects of basic ownership of the breed. It includes helpful information concerning the care of the Maltese, including coat care and grooming, selecting, and breeding. Bringing your Maltese puppy home and training your Maltese is also discussed extensively. Ms. Nicholas brings the breed to life with her knowledge and experience of many years as a author, judge, and dog authority.